Prairie Architecture

Critical Reviews

"The news was in the black glyphs on the supple birches' trunks," our poet notes in one typical moment of vision so sharp it's serrated. For Barron, all of it's news, all of it's breaking, and her dispatches from the field provide us blanket coverage. The prairie, the meadow, great lakes, rivers, Sonora, Canada, Cuba, you name it, these poems have worked that terrain, patiently undertaking the work of the imagination. And of memory—or as one astonishing poem sings its final wisdom: "I know: we lose some, / we lose some." This is a book that tallies its losses and its love of the world with equal force. One of many designs out of the mind of this architect is a series of imagined postcards that inhabit one place but reach back to another, so each poem's a bridge closing distances—sometimes great, sometimes between neighbors, or between here and the kitchen. Barron's the perfect poet to write these: armed with the photographer's eye, the traveller's restlessness, and the poet's imagined scrawl on the back of the card. She's out there, missing us, taking in the world she wants to share.

I just love these poems.

—Jamie D'Agostino, author of *Nude With Anything*; *Slur Oeuvre*; *Weathermanic*; and *This Much*

In Monica Barron's book of poetry, *Prairie Architecture*, there is a river that sends you back to where you came from. There are bridges, postcard poems about many places, and a series of linked sonnets. There is a tribute to Alice Neel, a poem about why we need ponds, a commentary on a father's death and another on hunters. I particularly enjoyed the poems that felt more personal, like "Polar Vortex", "Lana Turner All Day" and "Midsummer Songs," which concludes with this stanza:

> I would have guessed tonight
> would be clear: clouds the color
> of rhubarb, clean wind crossing
> the meadow. But winds have a way
> of changing. The leaves turn
> their silver undersides to me,
> my grandmother's favorite sign
> of rain. I know: we lose some,
> we lose some.

We do lose some, but we will always remember grandmother's signs of rain, and find beauty in this exquisite journey of a book.

—Lori Desrosiers, author of *The Philosopher's Daughter*, *Sometimes I Hear the Clock Speak* and *Keeping Planes in the Air* (Salmon Poetry).

Prairie Architecture

Poems by

Monica Barron

Golden Antelope Press
715 E. McPherson
Kirksville, Missouri 63501
2020

ISBN: 978-1-936135-80-6 (1-936145-91-7)

Library of Congress Control Number: 2020930141

Published by:
Golden Antelope Press
715 E. McPherson
Kirksville, Missouri 63501

Available at:
Golden Antelope Press
715 E. McPherson
Kirksville, Missouri, 63501
Phone: (660) 665-0273
http://www.goldenantelope.com
Email: ndelmoni@gmail.com

Acknowledgments:

- "Twenty-Year-Old-Memory of Kansas" appeared in *Poecology*, issue 3 (Summer 2013).

- "Hunting Song" and "Meditation from West of the River" appeared in *Naugatuck River Review*, the Winter 2012 issue, after being chosen as 3rd-place winner and finalist respectively in their narrative poetry contest.

- "Homage to Alice Neel" appeared in *The Chariton Review*.

- "Living In Larry's House" first appeared in *Times of Sorrow, Times of Grace*, an anthology of Great Plains women writers published by Backwaters Press.

- "Midsummer Songs" appeared in a slightly different version in *ArtWord Quarterly* published by Meristem Press.

- "An Anniversary of My Father's Death" first appeared in *Briar Cliff Review*.

- "Persimmons" first appeared in *The Lucid Stone Poetry Quarterly*.

- "Hottest Night So Far" first appeared in *Rosebud*, issue 58.

- "Why We Need Ponds" and "Jesus in Three Movements" are forthcoming in *EcoTheo Review*.

Contents

Prairie Architecture

Yellow Morning

Already a tremolo of sun through leaves
has begun and has a sound: Gerry
in the screen-porch playing cello
to a cornfield yellowing fast as, above
the blacktop, heat tremolos in silence
that yellows the ditches, the dogs covered in dust
that someone bellows for or maybe it's to
out of an anger that yellows his dried-up life,
his shed of gizmos, his rocking chair, his wife.

A distant dust cloud announces the mail.

Modern Beauty Center

Maggie said, "The small towns around here
    are all dead." They come to our town

to get their hair done, pay their taxes
    eat out. She doesn't need

a beauty shop, braids her long white
    hair every morning. It's Ella

she brought in, her sweet demented friend.
    In summer they garden on Ella's farm.

In winter they're in town at Maggie's place.

*

"It's Alzheimer's Day," Judy whispers
    as a tall silver-haired man

with "Junior" tooled into the back of his belt
    rises. His wife takes his hand.

"Senior" must be dead and gone.
    Why do I let her cut my hair?

She never cuts her own, lives at Gifford
    with horses, a garden, Mennonites around her.

*

… a December Sunday afternoon driving
    out near Gifford. Where the river bends

a yard with ratty pelts spread on the lawn
    ratty dog amongst them. Doe

the color of winter stubble moved through a field.
    Outside La Plata I passed a buggy

cab closed to keep wind out, balanced
  on its narrow black wheels. A group
of buggies clustered on the shoulder. Why?
  They've got to be home by dark. Later
high above my house geese flew
  in formation, dull braying
constellation in the winter sky.

*

She's right. Gifford, Milford, Elmer, and Ethel
  are dead, but there's a web of lives
out there maintained by something other than money
  changing hands. The sheriff calls
while Judy cuts my hair. One of the prisoners
  needs a haircut. "If he's still there
at four, I'll do it," she jokes. Our inmates tend
  to escape. I look across to the courthouse.
A bailiff walks a man in coveralls to jail.

Prairie Architecture

All their porches peel like mottled
tall sycamores' trunks.
Shutters peel blue painted
peaks peel white shaded
by massive catalpa with gnarly bark.
Those white blossoms won't last
in June wind. Old women
seem to know to hang sheets
and huge white panties dappled
by shadows of apple trees now.
Taller than the house old
oak and cottonwood are towers
of birds that fly fast over
rotted toppled fence. Garden
walls crumble into weedy
day lily beds. Brick
barbecues tilt into alleys,
mossy pyramids, wild mint
grown over their crumbling hearths.

Why We Need Ponds

To break the monotony of crops
we need ponds to be, on our home places,
the eyes that never close
as their grass lashes go to seed.

To collect what clouds drop
we need ponds, to let rain run
into rills, to let
grasses grow on their banks so that
rills don't become runnels,
so that snow melts and sinks in
as few things do.
We need ponds to let all waters
have a destination part of a cycle.

                              *

We need ponds to teach us patience.
When the water we prepared for doesn't come
we will have time to build a reef
the water rises and algae grows to cover
to stock the basin with fish and imagine them
trance-like with their lidless eyes and slight
correcting motions in the reef.
One day the pond will have become
a sanctuary for mating dragonflies
and coyotes tired of wandering the sandy beds
of old, high-walled creeks.

*

After such an effort
what might we become?
After changing the map
moving the horizon
of a place whose every dip
and roll every living
being thought it knew?
Once we have changed the weather
because it's not humid
enough in Greentop in August,
after changing the soundscape
so the whippoorwills and bluebirds
have migrating companions,
on the day the trees finally
see themselves in the pond's
mirror may we be
the reflection that fractures when
something lands on the pond's
placid surface breaking us
into a loving eye,
an awakened ear,
an open hand.

Hottest Night So Far

We were drinking in Marshall's dooryard
beneath the black walnut trees

where fields stretched to the reservoir
a mile beyond the blacktop's end.

I knew the purple sky was bouncing
off the reservoir's still surface.

Fields disappeared. Then the barn.
Even the bird feeders. House lights

coming on behind made us
silhouettes. *What fine shapes*

you all have! I wanted to say
but it didn't seem like the way

to fill the silence. I left it to Marshall
who told about a Greentop man

whose family reported him missing. He turned
up next day beneath three loads

of corn in his son's grain bin.
Findling's cows wandered up

from the creek. We could hear them bellow
beyond the barn's weak light,

Little calls of distress welling
up in the hot, still dark.

Kansas makes her think about

Kansas makes her think about
who it was she left behind:

Banks of wild, cream-colored iris
mark where a house used to be.

Bluestem, its roots like waterlilies, spreads
past the curve of the earth

turns red come October
and glistens, encrusted with ice—

the glacier must have been enormous.
In spring the flint hills are mottled

with burning fields. Skies are overcast,
seeing distance hard.

Meditation from West of the River

The house lights up, the doors and windows open,
we saw each other over the wreckage of dinner—
trout spines, candles burned to sockets,
red tulips doing backbends in a vase.
It was simple to motion you into the other room,
to sit in an armchair, begin a conversation
while the dogs howled up and down the alley
warning us away from our intentions.
I understood what it meant when you rose from your chair,
crossed the room, ran your hands through my hair.
I followed you back to the darkened kitchen,
put a hand on your shoulder to make you turn around.
As I closed my eyes to kiss you I was aware
of the gray the light was catching in your hair.

The light that caught the gray in your hair
was being caught by the crest of every wave,
tossed in a heap on the glistening shoals at our feet.
When I was a girl I walked this beach for miles,
waded into the waist-high waves to cool
my sun-burned skin. In pictures of that time
life looks uncluttered, the backdrop always a narrow
finger of land. Say what you want about memory,
it can be so clean. I remember us on the edge
of a pier while the sun slipped into the lake and the water
beat against the pilings. I was thinking a heart
could hold heat like sand after a sunset.
I was on the verge of trying to tell you this
when the sky began to darken, the sand turn cold.

The sky was darkening early. The ground turned cold.
But a steady heart can hold heat across
two states. Mine did. Light and color
sustained me: the silver of frost on rotting soybeans,
a carcass left to the dogs as the sun bled
the afternoon away. I learned nothing about
being alone. I would drive the highway to you
through sunsets lasting hours burning to a final
band of red at the horizon. I must
have been very young to think two days
of love could sustain me. I must have been
very young to think it was love at all.
Crossing the Mississippi late at night
I saw the ground fog rising to cover the road.

I saw the ground fog rising to cover the road
give way to frost. Say what you want about love,
it hates distance, hates the way a single
body cools in the purple air of a darkened
room. It hates ice, heads for open
water while I cling to shore.
I know you now. What you won't say, you won't
feel. I believe you are frightened by words, by the way
they call up things you meant to forget—
sand on a calf, distant banjo music,
a body turned away from you in sleep.
In two small rooms at the top of an old house
it can always be winter. Between two graying temples
it can always be silent. As long as you're not listening.

As long as you're not listening, it can always be silent,
but it's my way to listen to myself.
Today I lie on a sunny slope and tell
myself, Let go. What I hold is all
substance—a sweating glass, that blue shirt
you wore mornings while drinking coffee.
What I want is something I've never understood—
grace—that unearned, unasked-for peace.
One of these great plains evenings it might come
as I admire the blue of the darkening sky
against the shoe factory's worn brick.
Love might seem possible in that light,
the luck of those with a bit of sense and grace.
I would make peace with the way my heart works.

When I make peace with the way hearts work
I will call up Robin who asked me one night
in a hotel bar, *Where in this sad trafficking
do I go to find love?* I had no answer,
only took her hand and led her onto a terrace
where we shed our clothes and swam in a pool the sleeping
guests would never enter. When we went back
to the bar, a drag queen read my palm, saw *many
interruptions on my love line.* I figured
I was just like everybody else. But I'm not.
I want to love with enough intensity
to penetrate the losses that slake our hearts.
I want to help you live, to finally find
the synapse that connects the heart and mind.

Whatever it is that connects the heart and mind
it's at the mercy of memory. All evening I've walked
the west side of town in the lingering light
trying to recall what I felt for you
that evening in the cemetery when we found
Hoagy's grave. I wanted the sky to darken
just like it was in "Stardust," but it was early
summer. There was no stopping that light that bathed you
while you stood there humming that song. I know
that feeling, but it won't come back. The memory of
this last long winter on the plains
has my heart fast in its grasp.
It's dark. As I head for home with "Stardust" playing
in my head, I'm wishing you well, here
where the house lights are up, the doors and windows open.

The Big Lake Says

All afternoon people on the rocks
peered toward the spot where sky meets water.
I would not draw that line. Boats
puzzled in their slips. For hours
all was a grey sheen the gulls
circled in, blown-off shingles
in a funnel cloud. Crying
landing, their prints a dotted line
I erase. One of you walks
in this strange light turning to rain
between the sedge and the small dead
change I leave behind.

Ann and the Animas River

We choose our spirit guides. Mine
is the tall maple on my Missouri
lawn with the big pink X
on its trunk. I hear the saws
getting closer every day.
You choose eagle, for the way
it catches a draft down Animas Canyon
the same direction that river moves
the river of souls that claims the San Juan
Mountains as its source.

When you got to Durango you camped
at Lake Nighthorse filled by the Animas.
You saw the waters turned orange
by mine waste. Could it be the healing
place you sought when you left the last
soul-sucking town behind
for mountains? Follow the river, cleansing
its cargo in every canyon, passing
every ghost town on its way
to the Colorado. The big maple
is gone.

Bloodletting

I called my sister to wish her Happy Birthday.
She said she'd been up since five, awakened
by gunshots on the marsh the first day
of duck season. Late mornings soon
there'll be deer strapped to vehicles
in the Northtown Café's gravel lot.

We have to talk about Mom, my sister said.
Do we ever stop? She's ready to put
our father in a nursing home. He doesn't
know her, and she can't lift him anymore.
I said, Let her do it. A woman at work
got a call that both her parents were dead.
She went home to find her father had shot
her mother, bed-ridden five years, and then
himself. His cancer had come out of remission
and he couldn't care for her anymore. I never
saw the room, of course, but I imagine
cleaning it. Let her do it. Maybe it's time.

Maybe it's time to admit that the bloodletting
now rivals my childhood in Detroit.
When Hoffa disappeared, his adopted son
"Chuckie" O'Brien was asked by reporters
about the blood-soaked backseat of his car.
A very big fish, he said. I recently caught
a very big fish.

Fare Well

An ad in *The Daily Express* said,
Come by dark. Leave the blacktop.
Go down into Sugar Creek Forest.

                            *

No shoulder on the road here.
We left the truck half in a tangle
of weeds, ripening berries dusted
by the road and took the steep path
below the house.
                            Already it was dark.
Someone tilled and planted once
this large clearing bounded by the jagged
silhouettes of trees.
                            In the light
from two tall braziers burning charcoal,
burning myrrh, my eyes adjusted slowly.
It might have been *him*, that shrouded figure
lying on the bier, not some plaster effigy.

This is our send-off for Jim,
                local nursery owner, expert grower,
                county-wide gab man.

                            *

Jim kept his hat on, part
custom of the county, part vanity:
He was balding.
                            Short, small-
butted, slightly paunchy, always in jeans
and slightly tinted wire-rimmed glasses.

One Friday evening we were sipping beer
at a table by the window watching the sky

change by looking down the alley between
the two-story bricks across the street.
Jim asked me how my poetry was going
and said he'd been reading Ferlinghetti.
It seemed to him Larry and his friends
had proclaimed themselves a movement.
                                                    And kept on moving.
That's what you have to do, he said, rocking
back on his chair, rocking forward.
But then get moving.

                                    *

I never got moving that way.
Then Jim had a stroke and couldn't talk.
And the bar's tattered miracles
of taxidermy—
                              wide-mouth bass,
wild turkey, moose in sunglasses,
mangy, bandana-wearing coyote—
some nights seemed they would outlast us all.

                                    *

Pens in hand, we approached the plaster effigy
to write our good byes. "Look for me under
your bootsoles…" his wife wrote; "I stop some where
waiting for you." Someone thrummed a drum.

Then the bier was lifted onto a high
pyre, the effigy's mask still lit
by braziers at its head and foot. One son
lit the pyre, east and west. I saw
to the trees along Sugar Creek,
saw, finally, who was there. It burned
for hours. They say his sons slept in the clearing.
Toward dawn, did they shift in their slumber?
Ember turned to ash on a breeze.

This moment I'm living in

"This moment you're living in is a poem."

Naomi Shihab Nye

She can make a poem out of anything.
A saucer of olives on the Gaza Strip.
Me, I'm porch-sitting in a rocker

whose cane seat is breaking, leaving me
to sit like the old woman in Candide
who lost a buttock blockaded in a castle,

the food running out in "the best of all possible worlds."
Down the street, beyond the movie theatre
there's a sunset going on I can hardly see.

Across the way the Mennonite landlord tore up
the concrete from the sidewalk to the porch,
intending, I guess, to build a ramp. For here

doubled over with a cane his new
tenant struggles to walk up the slope
of the lawn. Two men who don't know what

to do stand slightly behind and to each side
in case she falls back down the slope.
At a moment like this she could really use

two EMTs to drive up and put her
on a stretcher and take her inside.
Instead it takes an hour for her to get up

the slope. And I'm glad it's dark because
it looks like her skirt is hiked up

in back so she can walk.

The three steps up take another half hour
during which she seems to be lying
on the steps grabbing up at the railing.

I'm worried she's bruising herself but the men
don't seem worried. The dog is barking. She calls it
"Lucy" and I'm wondering if she lives

alone and if she could get out of that house
if it caught fire. One man calls her "mama,"
but he might be her husband, maybe he'd pull her

out. I wish this poem were more lovely.
The old woman makes it up the steps
and sits down. Lucy comes out.
And Ashley from next door who is sometimes

afraid of the neighbors comes over and sits.
It's dark now, so I hear their voices
but can't see much. After a while the old man

says, *Are you ready for me to help you up?*
She's not so he says, *watch the damn dog, then*
and goes in. What could make this poem lovelier

now that we're all in our busted chairs
waiting to fall to the deck and we've missed
a sunset at the edge of town where sometimes

the distant clouds look like mountains is some
quiet, please. The kind that makes you aware
that everyone's breathing in time to the cicadas.

Sometimes your only muse is
The Minimalist

Start heating a skillet, warming
water for pasta. *Take a shallot...*
(Oh really, Mark Bittman? Take an onion.)
Chop it with garlic, sauté until soft.

Add some Aleppo red pepper
But try not to think about war and Syria.
Peel the butternut squash you've been saving
next to your cardboard wine cellar.

Cube the squash (see why you're not
drinking yet?) Then add the squash
and diced tomatoes with their juice.
Cover the thing and let it simmer

—not boil—til the squash is tender
and the wine takes the edge off you
because you do, sometimes, have
an edge. Make sure there's a crappy little

kitchen radio playing something
great on *Performance Today*
that makes you feel a little wistful
you missed Candide at Wolftrap back in

June, but soldier on, especially
if there are children to be fed.
Chop some parsley if you're going
vegan tonight or grate a bit

of aged cheese. Add salt and pepper.
Cook some pasta–Ditali
is good, but don't be precious about it.
Get 'er done. Warm some bowls.

Assemble this lovingly. *Performance Today*
is making you tear up and the sauce
so bright—all orange and red—is a big
gong going off inside you.

An Anniversary of My Father's Death

Midday I stop at a crossroads gas station
near St. Meinrad Abbey. We could see it
there above the town and the fields,
the woman who pumped my gas and sold me melon
and I. All day I drove the two-lane through
the corn, grown up high to the road.
That was the horizon, not the distant
gray line beyond the winter stubble.

Absence is not the dark thing I imagined.
It's cayenne lilies sprouting from grassy ditches,
turtles sunning themselves, old women
pumping gas and selling melons. Strong
light over the fields. At dark I put
the headlights on and drove that tunnel of corn.

Silkie

After a Norwegian folktale

I saw them offshore frolicking
(I never use that word) and wondered

What would it be like to…?
When I thought they'd gone, she appeared.

And I learned what it's like to.
The skin she sloughed off, I never found.

She knew how to do everything
in a silence that never broke

into song. Fiercely attached
to the body of water she grew up on,

in, she sometimes slipped and said,
she was a homebody. One day the sun

shone hot on every stone. She took
my hand and said, "I'll teach you to swim

in the foam. I swam into the channel,
flipped over on my back. While I

was taken with the shape of a cloud
she slipped away. Legend has it

I must shed seven tears
at the water's edge to bring her back.

The Which? of July

I surfaced this morning
at a fashionably early hour
itching to pledge allegiance
to something that wasn't
a normative discourse.
It could have been the feel
of the freshly painted porch
under my bare feet,
the flag-less flagpole
at Village 76
or my sneaky satisfaction
at Facebook plaintively checking
my location once again:
is it really Mary Immaculate Church?

If your phone rings before
you finish listening to this poem
realize you have a certain power:
it could just be Claire McCaskill
interrupting her way to agency
with a red-white-and-blue robocall
that insinuates we might think alike
if only you wouldn't think so hard.
But she has other paths
to agency. Poets don't.
Next time give her that dial-a-bell-hooks-
quote number and stay
in this lawn-chair moment
while grass-fed beef glares red
before it turns to brown
and the barbecue smoke gives way
to gunpowder over the buckling concrete
of this queer little town.

Midsummer Songs

1

All day I live beneath
a canopy of oak and pine.
Bird-song, rain, and light filter through.
At sunset I walk down
to the meadow to holler my truths
to the blue, blue distant hills.
The wind blows them back.

2

Days full of light
shortening ever so slightly.
A yellow flower changes
to a dark green phallus.
Night comes earlier
beneath these trees.
I row my dinghy out
onto open water to buy
myself some time.

3

I would have guessed tonight
would be clear: clouds the color
of rhubarb, clean wind crossing
the meadow. But winds have a way
of changing. The leaves turn
their silver undersides to me,
my grandmother's favorite sign
of rain. I know: we lose some,
we lose some.

Hunting Song

i.

All year the silent men of Adair County
drive alone, giving the one-finger
salute to vehicles passing on the blacktop.
No singing in the cab. No wild arguments
with themselves. Maybe they talk the morning
deer season opens, orange hats
clustered in an old Dodge Ram
on their way to the woods, their separate stands.

Maybe they talk waiting in line at the smokehouse
wanting to bring the kill in fast because
November's warm. They look in the bed
of the truck ahead. No one
shuts a slain buck's eyes. They don't
remark except to say the line is long.

ii.

Hunters are everywhere! They're down the road
camping out, tearing ruts in the clay
winding down to the river. They've found Audrey's
Place at Queen City Junction, in an abandoned
gas station painted-up. Customers
peeling off a layer never fail to note
Audrey's wearing a tube top, her amber mane
barely constrained in a pile on her head,
her eyeliner calligraphied to her temples.
Her old man's been in the kitchen frying since Nam,
trying not to watch her flirt with the guys in camo
whose money's green. I eat my gooseberry cobbler,
thinking she might sit down to play the spinet
covered with doilies and faceless Amish dolls.

iii.

We call this place on the river "Archangel,"
Twain's nickname for Henry Clay Dean
who signed his writings from Rebel's Cove just up
the river's last five unchanneled miles.
Huge sycamores wrapped in ropey ivy
line its banks. Oh, they look like tremendous
wings, those bits of white water, ruffled
feathers. You can float the twisting river
here and end up nearly where you started.

If only the river had taken Audrey under
its mighty wing. She might never have shot
her husband in the kitchen after close.
The sign still says Audrey's Place, but
how empty, how silent the place with her gone.

The State of Midwest Passenger Rail Travel

The train man's gums
                    gleam in the afternoon sun
Even with a belt
                    he can barely keep his pants up
But the flaps are up
                    on his winter hat this November Day

The train is three hours late for a five-hour trip
Freight, he tells us, gets first clearance on this line
every time

The train comes
                    and there are lots of seats
but no heat in the car
                    People must have gotten off
and started walking
                    to Chicago

Postcard:
The Mabel Dodge Luhan House

Caption: The Mabel Dodge Luhan House in Taos, NM

Of Mabel, Gertrude wrote, *There is that which is in time.*

Up canyon from the square is her adobe

in time with the pueblo and the Penitente morada.

So much flying to and from the odd collection of bird houses.

There is no occupancy that isn't fleeting.

So much flying. That isn't fleeing.

Even the water in the acequia.

The grass has intentions.

The mountain, a suggestion.

Jesus in Three Movements

I

Before the border walls
there were mission walls.
At Tumacacori they crumbled
to Sonoran sand
and the fossilized pits
of Fr. Kino's peaches.
Jesus replants the mission
orchard with the oldest
root stock he can find.
In downtown Tucson yards
abuelas keep alive
the old world stock—
black mission figs.
From cuttings to seedlings Jesus
nurses the trees, plants them
near the old acequia,
wraps their slender trunks
to protect them.

II
Layers of checkpoints at Nogales,
first, out on the interstate,
a sun-baked shipping container
their makeshift detention center.
North of the crossing people wrapped
in blue tarps slept on the highway.

Jesus warned us away from vendors
selling home-canned goods
and plastic bags of quesadilla.
He sang corridas as our bus
wound its way up the mountain,
sang us past a huge truck
overturned on the road's edge,
sang us by the smoldering fires
left by people going north
through the Sonoran desert.

At Santiago de Cocospera
he shook his head at pieces
of the crumbling church stored in a shed
while the tin nailed to what was left
of Cocospera tore off
in a hot wind. Acres
of white plastic greenhouses
below us in the valley. From where
comes the water?

III

You don't know what richness *is*,
Jesus said, knocking on
an old woman's door. She kept
keys to the white-washed mission,
San Ignacio Sonora. He wanted
us to see her walled garden—
quince fig lime lemon.
Taste this, he said, pulling a lime
from a branch, cutting it into
slivers. Old world stock planted
along an acequia. A screened
kitchen around a huge copper
pot to cook the quince down.
Taste *this*, he said, shaving a block
of quince paste into small bites.
Parakeets and parrots chattered
in their cages. These are
the keys to the kingdom.

Patrick's Poem

Because the Sangre de Cristo can never surround them
completely, there are these walls

Grainy, rounded, rock-rose adobe
of the very earth the houses sit on, walls

Calle Elena no wider than an alley
every house but hers inside a wall

At one end the arroyo's banks of blooming sage
willow, clover wait for water to wall

At the other end the Santa Fe River sometimes
moved between crumbling quarried stone walls

When her brother died, the grief could not
be held within any sort of wall

To see that the Rio Grande was cradled in a mountainous
bowl, she climbed a mountain's warm wall

If only she'd had his ashes then to release
into clouds never caught long by these mountains

For My Brother

Living in Larry's House

My neighbors see my house lights on late
across the fields. I've got drapes, but never
draw them. The blacktop's two miles away.
When Larry died, I bought this farm cheap,
moved here alone, and figured Larry'd died,
a victim of our customs. Out here sometimes
a family picks one boy to do its chores
and never sends him to school. That boy ends up
as Larry did, an old bachelor, mad
in a rotting house after his mother died.
He scared the neighbors, driving the rutted roads
too fast, killing their cats and dogs. The chores
are no problem here: I haul water,
beat the wood chucks gnawing through the floor,
can tomatoes. But nights are trouble. I keep
a glass of sipping liquor near and stare
from my ex-husband's photo to
that deep band of red on the horizon
when all the life that's going to stir
is making its last move.

Persimmons

She taught me this: to go walking early, collecting
persimmons from sidewalks, lawns when just a touch
of frost entered Indiana overnight.
I never saw how tall persimmon trees were.
I kept my eyes on the ground, scavenging fruit
before the birds wised-up, before the cars
slid through crosswalks slick with mashed orange flesh.
We went for coffee when our hands got cold.

So many years later the ways of an old love persist,
one more rite that nets not belief, but the flesh
of something small, ripe, sweet. At night
I collect persimmons from the group-home lawn,
pour a drink and put them through a mill
whose motion convinces me: winter's coming on.

Feeding Tom's Sheep

i

By the time we cross the dooryard
and reach the barnyard gate they have moved
into the pasture. One brown tup
in a flock of old ewes munching wizened grass.

Who are we to them? He asked us
to feed his sheep, to stoop entering the rusted
barn, grab a bale and limp to the rake
spread the hay and pump water

into a claw-foot tub. I tell
the lone chicken, *This barn looks blue
in wan December light.* It's warm,
easy to take a deep breath of sheep

and watch the sky striate
into purples. Closing my eyes that night
there are no hills rolling to creeks,
no sheep stock-still, no lights in the barn.

ii

The ping of sleet on corrugated tin   the first
huge drops imprinting Hazel Creek's wide sandy
bed   Sleet falls on pin oaks   still holding their leaves

on black oaks that dropped their leaves into ravines
cut into clay by rain and sleet that falls on the splendid
cedars bending   as they are coated   bending as we all

begin to bend   Every limb   every wet head will bow
Sleet falls on the sheep   on the grass the sheep eat
on you   on me   on the sheep   on the dead ewe

iii

Good King Wenceslaus looked out
on the feast of Stephen. But it hadn't rained ice.
I have my own grim carol to sing—
A ewe down in the barnyard, her carcass a huge hive
of ice-encrusted wool and bloated flesh, her bottom
jaw gnawed, her still pink gums and teeth exposed.
Grim carol, the crackle of branches struggling to move
in their icy coats, the bark of a shovel striking
a watering tub's frozen surface, the thud
of heaved ice hitting the ground.

Who are we to them now who don't retreat
as we approach, who hover and stare
as we push them away to fill the rake
whose breath mingles with ours
in the cold steamy air?

The Cold One

I hugged the frozen sheets as I took them
down from the line, smiled doing
one more thing you taught me. Sometimes
even the neighbor kids mock
my hanging the laundry out.

Don't you have a dryer? one yelled.

The sun's free, I yelled back.

No, it's not, she said coming
closer, *you gotta pay god.*

God isn't about money,
I said smugly, as if I know
what god's about, as if he sits down
at my table at Happy Hour
and lets me buy him a cold one.

Yes, he is, she said. *And you gotta pay.*

Maybe I am paying today when the wind
is a thousand, cold unintelligible
tongues lashing me awake.

To go inside too soon would be
to miss their consolations.

The night after you died a storm
blew up Lake Michigan into
the harbor where I sat staring

at boats shrouded in plastic, snow
piling up around them as if
the lake deposited strange icy
detritus for me to weep over
while you were reduced to ash.
I know what I whispered to you
as the cold crept up your body.
I will not say it again.   Damn
the planets shining in the evening sky.
This whole frozen world is what you left me.

Are You My Mother?

Camille sitting next to Lyla in her high chair
reads Seuss' *Are You My Mother?* aloud.

Of course, Lyla's interested—a beautiful woman
with long dark hair, a familiar voice, saying things

others regard as a story. Lyla
watches big-eyed, raises her eyebrows, but doesn't

know she quickened in Camille's womb
that Camille played cello all through the quickening

then gave her to this couple, present at her birth
who are now her life. Camille laughs as she reads.

It could be the laugh of a woman wondering if
she is a mother or was, but is now a well-wisher,

not a bird searching for its baby.
Lyla is not confused about who mother is:

mother is here. Camille and the cello come
and go. Here for the most ordinary

of moments: reading aloud to a child learning
sounds signify: mother is a body
with meaning attached.

She asked about my coat

Of a gnarly blue and sand tweed that looks alive—like seed heads
of dune grass, morel spores and fern sprouting on a blanket. Knee-
length with two patch pockets in front just big enough for me to
jam my hands into. It looks handmade, the buttons and their
holes just a little crooked. I found it on a rack one rainy after-
noon we wandered shops behind the dunes in New Buffalo. And
the lining! The blue satin slid over my sun-burned skin. I knew
the way snow would blow down the lake. I could face January
wrapped in the rainy choice of that afternoon.

Homage to Alice Neel

I. Colwyn, Pennsylvania

Our street had been a pear orchard. Such beauty
in the spring. But we had no artist to paint it
or the man who once exposed himself at a window.
We lost so many things by being who
we were: not a writer among us after the grocer
died and his wife committed suicide.

Summers I willed my blood
to stop in my veins. When I began to paint
I avoided yellow light, blue shadow
and picnics on the grass. I learned that the nose
was very little bone, mostly gristle.
I studied with Paula Balano, whose husband wrote
I love you, Paula across their apartment walls.
Women terrified me; boys always chased me.

II. Havana, 1924: the first marriage

Picasso had torn the world to pieces.
Peacocks walked in Carlos's garden. I painted
every day to understand that light.
Days were hot. Nights we'd take a bus
to the outskirts of town to sketch the Afro-Cubans
dancing and disappearing into the bushes.

Understand that his family was not bourgeois.
They had owned provinces, paid men to cut
their sugar cane by night. His mother was dressed
by slaves. Imagine eating fried banana
in a garden with walls a yard thick.
I had a child. We returned to the States; "all the little
threads of my heart and spirit were somehow connecting
themselves with the classic beauty of washington bridge."

III. Threnody

And then my first daughter died. My husband left me.
I breathed grief and wanted to die. My brother
found me with my head in the oven. I came to,
an orderly bent over me saying, *It's no use, baby.*
On my ward the knives and forks were rubber
so I smashed a glass and tried to eat the shards.
Each night beyond the nimbus of the lamp
beneath my bed, I tried to die. Finally
I began to draw. The doctor asked to sit
for me. I said, *I won't draw you,*
You're the enemy. I remember a terrace with wisteria.
I remember my volition being frozen,
Long afternoons in tubs of hot water,
The doctor saying, *Why don't you look in the mirror*
    and get well?

IV. The Return to Real Life

I never went to Teaneck to live with my sister.
I headed for the village: one free meal
a day until the government hired me as
an easel painter. I wanted paint and history
on every canvas: Wobblies, Puerto Ricans,
a family living under an overturned car:
I'd paint them in north light. It never changes.

Once a sailor I brought home slashed
all of my paintings, all of the portraits outlined
in blue or black. For a long time after that
my own face bored me. And I knew that night I'd kissed
my husband hard and said, *I'm never going
to change*, I'd told the truth. To prove it, I painted
the Fuller Brush man in north light, unchanging.

The Saturday Train from Boston to Providence

A girl up the car wears a paper hat that says "bra stuffer."
What's the story? I ask the young guy next to me
in my best rust-belt accent. *Lingerie Show at Faneuill Hall*,
he murmurs. Hope she got a door prize for that one.
Her friend's hat says, "Future Hooters Waitress."

I'm hoping she just means while she's in college.
But what do I know about goal-setting when you're thirteen?
Right about then I may have wanted to be
a high school band director or to follow my sister
and her pot-smoking draft-dodging boyfriend to Canada.

A woman four rows up works on a laptop, chews
a bagel while on the phone arranging a cab
to take her to a prison to see a man
the girl next to her refers to as "dad."
They get off at the next stop as it starts to snow.

O Massachusetts! Your wet winter woodiness out
the train window distracts me from the goals
my financial advisor thinks are close to the fearful
surface of a woman my age: peace on earth? Nah.
A trip to the wineries of New Zealand? Look,

birches like the ones in the Frost poem a boy would dream
of bending down to ride upon. They distract me
from the jagged Rhode Island coast I am heading toward.

Something Is Certainly Ending

—Miles of corn stubble, nothing more than turkey clustered
                              in the cleared fields.

Finally, a buggy dropping Amish children at the top of a road
        reddened by a sun so huge it shone
                                    from Indiana to the Tetons.

We're driving north to Elk River New Year's Eve. The moon's face
        misted, cleared, near the Minnesota border.

—The cabin on the wooded slope of a frozen lake.
                    Ice moans.

She can't shovel the snow off the roof anymore. Her hip aches.
She can't get out of chairs, maintain her balance. She waits winter out.

We talked until we dozed, silent in front of Times Square on tv,
        its manholes welded shut, trashcans gone.

When we slept we slept in a pine paneled room with a cold floor.
        She'd made the quilt—
The Drunkard's Way. It took her 25 years to finish.

At midnight, distant fireworks or gunshots.
Flying squirrels clinging to the feeders swaying in the wind.
Once there were loons in the summer. Now she listens to them on tape
        as she tries to sleep.

—sunlight reflected off that frozen lake all day, up through the bare
                trees and the cedars on the slope.

Out on the ice you told me when she drove the school bus
             she would bring your skates, let you out
                 across the lake to skate home fast.
There was a day the ice cracked all around you and you almost didn't
make it.

She was probably watching the nuthatches now
                  running head-first down the cedars
Not us far out on the ice, reading its fissures,

Not thinking about her aching hip, or how there used to be elk at Elk
River.

—when we came back in May she wasn't there,
            lay near death in a Twin Cities hospital.

The news was in the black glyphs on the supple birches' trunks
         the bridge out over the St. Francis,
            the long foggy detour to the cabin that night
               through potato fields yielding to subdivisions
                  at the edge of the dunes and back
a cabin where someone had done the dishes but not filled the bird feed-
ers.

What Grief There Is

[*Numbers are the order in which they were composed.*]

1

Frankenthaler died. I saw *The Times* this morning.
    There comes a point when you're grieving when
    you at least can notice others are dying too.

8

On the 12th floor she felt eye to eye with planes, not
    the Mississippi below with its thin skin of ice.
    Thin-skinned above she watched the pantomime
    below on Kellogg Boulevard.

3

It snowed on Kim Jong-il's funeral. A limousine
    topped with his portrait approached the palace
    followed by another with a snow-covered coffin
    on its roof.

7

Apricot to lavender to purple to blue. Moving points
    of light revealed themselves to be planes land-
    ing. Where were the ashes?

4

Journalists asked if the people's grief was chore-
    ographed. Thousands crying and wailing in snowy
    streets as the cortege passed. Cold question.

11

When he came down from Manitoba New Year's
    Day it was the bees we talked about. Colony
    collapse. You thought, *family collapse.*

9

Year-old tsunami debris washed up in British Columbia.
    Someone's grief from the other side of the Pa-
    cific Rim. No bodies.

6

The ashes are in a blue glass jar that she loved. The
    jar still warm when he picked them up. The lake
    froze before we could bear to scatter them.

2

What we leave behind matters. She left "Moun-
    tains and Sea." Color that didn't refer, it evoked.
    Green like sun shining on pines.

10

Spread her on the lake in the presence of loons. In
    the presence of nesting eagles. Migrating sand-
    hill cranes. The squirrels who outlived her.

5

On BBC silent video of crying children in pastel
    jackets laying white flowers at a wall in Pyongyang.

We Were Lied To

From the Blue Water Bridge, Lake Huron looked
As if there were enough to go around.

The sound of the lake released at the tap
Was hopeful as it hit the basin,
Georgian Bay arriving to quench our thirst.

When the water began to run orange
We enquired and were told
We're drinking the Flint River now
To save a few bucks. True.

But we were lied to when we were told
there was no danger. And for two more years
while the water bills kept coming and our
houses lost their value we were
lied to. Presidential candidates
came and went as we hauled water
and taught our children to sponge-bathe
in a place so rich with fresh water
we'll be building pipelines to the desert.

The cold blue truths we swam in
until our teeth chattered have become
the brown sludge dulling
our bright-eyed children.

A Parking Lot, A Palm Tree, Night

Huge palm fronds against a dark
sky look like shadows

out the shuttle window. Marooned
in a dark parking lot

lined with more palms, their crowns lit
from below by amber lights,

the hotel and Hooters of Boca Raton.
It is I who am marooned

in this way station for the many
kinds of weary wandering

the world. The outside tables are empty.
Inside, would I be distracted by

Boca Raton's biggest breasts?
Would I miss the Applebee's-

Chili's chain-pub décor
or Diane Reeves in heavy

rotation with the Rat Pack? There was
nothing I would label

a hooter in Hooters that night,
nothing over-sized,

not the gin and tonic, not
the fish tacos, not

the perfectly unremarkable breasts
of the woman in the tight

orange scoop-necked tee and tiny
shorts who brought the modest

check which I will not file
for reimbursement.

Postcard: Cabo Rojo

Caption: on Puerto Rico's southwest coast. Known for its
diverse ecosystem including the Corozo Salt Flats, man-
grove forests, limestone cliffs, and coral reefs

It's an end of the world

There is no line between sky and water

The line between
water and land draws itself
redraws itself and disappears

in the boil of sand and water
in acres of salt flats traversed
by rutted red dirt roads

Sea birds ride wind currents
along the cliffs An onshore breeze
blasts ashore A handful of people
look over the edge of the world, afraid

Outside Mayaguez

Winding up the road to the parador
we don't know where to look first—to clusters
of thick bamboo tall enough to under-
story giant palms? Or to that pile
of rubble with a satellite dish on top?
In the vivero, black netting filters
July sun from coffee trees still in pots.
Up the mountain mature coffee grows
beneath whatever trees were there first—
shade-grown, bird habitat preserved.

The parador is quiet when we drive in.
Chickens range. El perro will be our guide.
Ventanas and doors closed against mid-day heat.
To one side of a shaded courtyard an open-
air sitting room and restaurant.
Two men playing chess until lunch—
café con leche, rice and beans, tostones.
El perro rests on cool tile while
we eat, then leads us down a jungle trail.
Bamboo mulch, plantains, lizards. One hundred
inches of rain per year. Growth and rot.
A bit of an old self drips to the jungle floor.

Her blue mask, her yellow wall

In an old barrio near
the Ponce playa, Miguel
made her a blue mask
to ward off harm. It hangs
on her yellow wall, looks

beyond the ventanas
where the wandering dogs scratch
all night, the coqui call.
Palm fronds rustle.
Lizards hang on the screen.

Polar Vortex

3

I woke to crows and a radio murmuring in another room.
Your room. I'm under every blanket, quilt, afghan I could
find, assigned to the guest room. I am a guest.
You sleep under "The Drunkard's Way," the heaviest quilt your
    mother
ever made. It took her twenty-five years. I saw my breath
in your chilly basement and wondered why your pipes hadn't
frozen. They must run deep, deeper than mine (which used to be
    ours)
buried in the Missouri clay. Why the cold hadn't stalled
my lungs when I drew my first breath stepping off the train,
I don't know. Something about this wall color—moss, lichen,
spruce—pulls me out of this moment.

2

The fecund tangle of the garden
an earlier owner planted—I won't
see it. I see the wizened shapes
of the anchor plants standing in snow—
echinacea, clematis, trumpet
vine—foregrounding the charred shape
of your neighbor's bungalow. The power
is still on and we watch
the house wondering if someone
is still living there. Twenty-
six below last night.
The flagstone path narrows every snow.

1

My gloves were only good for fifteen minutes at twenty below.
On the slick, windy sidewalk you pointed out the Ethiopian
restaurant you take out from, a mattress store called House of
        Sleep
and a bar that holds a weekly meat raffle. While I shopped
for gloves in TJ Maxx a pipe burst. A clerk calmly
grabbed a cart, pulling socks off their racks as the water
began to pool. The fire department arrived without a wrench.
The ice piled up outside. But that one clerk kept at it. No flood
would destroy her cold confounding world. Not yet.

0

The wall color was spruce, the color
of the first Minneapolis room
we slept in on the River's east
bank. There were curtains over
the back stairs door we opened when
there were barely lilacs. All
the touches then were full of hope
and now they say, *I know you.*
Stay right where you are. Now
there's a faucet running somewhere
in a small steady stream
to keep everything from freezing.

Twenty-year-old Memory of Kansas

Chase County, near Cottonwood Falls—
huge, flinty swellings in the earth
distant horizon line that is only a curve
never an edge. A 360-degree view.
Clouds like petroglyphs, bluestem
dried red, glistening in its icy crust.
A coyote, head down, crosses the blacktop.
My elation.

In Praise of Netting

When you first saw the netting over the garden
it was early summer, wrens plucking tender
green shoots of plants for their young.
You praised the way I'd bought pipe and joints,
made a hoop of netting. *Temporary*, you thought.

I could already hear earth cracking
as the tendrils inclined up, wove themselves
into the netting above the cages, blossomed,
fruited Purple Cherokee, Lemon Boy
suspended in a trellis of vine and net.

Below ground roots entangled, drew sustenance.
The vines withered woven into the netting.
At the first big snow I took it down
tossed it into a corner where it wouldn't
blow away. I wondered if come spring
I would have the patience to pull the rot
from the netting and use it again.

Easter morning ankle-deep in wet
leaves, unthreading dead vine from netting
I began again the weave of plant and place.
Already the bugs were murmuring *again,*
bend to the soil. Weave and be part of the weave.
Showering later I noticed something had bit me
on the neck.

Postcard: The Book Cliffs

Caption: The Book Cliffs extend nearly 200 miles from south
of Vernal, Utah east to the Colorado border. They are
cretaceous sandstone formations varying in altitude from
8,000 to 4500 feet.

If you call it a book, I'll want to read it, left to right,
line by line the earth's business, a 200-mile-long
sandstone page.

But we seem to be driving right to left at 70 miles
per hour.

Never toward the books, never down a tire-flattening,
axle-breaking path to box canyons full of inscrutable
petroglyphs.

The guidebooks say *isolation* and *solace* for those
who open the book.

The rest imagine dragging a finger along the spines
on a library shelf, never grabbing hold of one.

Thanks, Moab

So all along time has been our invention
a distraction from eternity, that thread
with no beginning or end, earth and love
on earth the part we can see. So we have
time, place, and love.

                    She took us to
the Chama River valley, the White Place O'Keefe
could see from her bed and studio. Then we had place,
absence, objects, time. But what kind of time?
Her long love for the rocks made visible.

We have long love for a woman made visible—
that photo of a mother holding a daughter's
hand while the son takes a picture.
Now we have love, no hands, only photos
and a hole in our hearts the size of the Delicate Arch.

                              For Sharon, Cole, Shawn

Lana Turner All Day

I was watching *Imitation of Life*

when a friend rang my doorbell. Lana

was trying to become a movie star

when she lost her daughter at Coney Island

and didn't know what to do.

This was before amber alerts.

A homeless black woman, all her

belongings neatly packed in a suitcase,

with a daughter who could pass as white

found Lana's daughter. Lana took

the woman and her daughter in.

I know, I know: movie stars go

to the beach every day and pick up

the homeless. Why is this of interest?

Lana wasn't a star yet,

but this woman believed in her,

kept the apartment and Lana's wardrobe

and addressed envelopes at the kitchen

table for money. Somehow they got

by together. My doorbell rang.

I turned Lana off. She's

not real. My friend is.

[Interlude]

I turned Lana back on.

Now in *The Rains of Ranchipur*

she was a spoiled rich bitch

who fell in love with Richard Burton

spray painted to look Indian.

The turban helped. He played an unselfish

doctor who cared for the untouchables

—a real Mother Theresa. Lana

didn't love her British husband.

He didn't love her back. Richard

tried not to fall in love

with her. He knew she was trouble.

But she did visit the untouchables

with him one night. He must have

looked into her shriveled-up soul

and seen a loving, unselfish

non-narcissistic bottle

blonde and fallen in love. Meanwhile

Lana's husband figures out

what's up. But Richard saves him

from a man-eating tiger. There was

a moment when I saw the writer

could have written a Hemingway ending.

(In *The Short Happy Life*

of Francis Macomber the wife picks

up the gun when the wild thing

attacks her estranged husband but ends up

shooting her husband. The hunting guide

she favored suggests it wasn't an accident.)

One night Lana, her husband, Richard,

and Lana's old alcoholic

boyfriend, Fred MacMurray are at

a party when an earthquake strikes.

Richard must go to the untouchables.

He's gone for days during which

a dam breaks, flooding everything.

Lana battles fever in weird

pajamas at the American Mission.

She almost dies. She wonders why

her doctor-lover never comes.

An American woman running the mission

tells her it's because of the river,

the flood. She knows Americans well.

When Richard finally shows up

he tells Lana it wasn't the river.

It was the many, the people. He chose

the many over her. Always

he would. There were seismic shifts

going on in Lana's shriveled-up heart.

Looking for Democrats in Novinger, MO

We asked for signs
the signs were sent
Leonard Cohen

I
They gave us bottled water, a list
of addresses and names trending Democrat
then waved goodbye. Not my idea
of how to help Hillary or the county Dems
who suddenly seemed to be run
by young white men from St Louis
who sent us to a town whose name
they couldn't pronounce—which meant they couldn't
visualize what they were asking us
to do. Still we went up and down
rolling gravel roads, lined
with grass, Queen Anne's lace and chicory
six feet tall. Houses without
addresses, mailboxes clustered elsewhere.
Wandering hens, doddering dogs.
Our sunscreen melting off in the late-morning heat.
They knew we weren't Jehovah's Witnesses.
An occasional truck passed and left us
in a cloud of dust that wasn't trending
Democrat.

II

Election night. I'm at a Park n Fly
near Kansas City International
watching planes take off and land
while a bunch of white people chain smoke.
They're not trending Democrat.
At the desk a South Asian man
plays the role of host uneasily.
On tv Brian Williams anchors his ship
of awkward silence. At two I wonder
if I should sleep at all. A crowd waits
under the glass ceiling at Javits Center
but no one appears. *There is a crack,*
a crack in everything. The same old crack.

Later I watch her concession speech in O'Hare.
While people try to read her blouse
and Bill's tie—"Purple is red + blue"—
I listen instead to her words: "We have seen
that our nation is more deeply divided than
we thought." As I get on the plane, there is
a crack in me. *That's how the light gets in.*

III

O Canada…you let us in politely,
wished us a good conference, didn't question
our documents, ravish our luggage, mock our election
results, or grab us by the pussy before
we left the airport. You could tell some of us
were hurting. The older Black feminists said,
we've been here before. Let's just get to work.
Others said, *No business as usual.* But nobody
said *no business.*

Thank you, Leonard, your death bumped Donald
and Hillary off page one of *The Globe and Mail.*
And CBC played tribute: *Forget your perfect
offering.* Oh we will, Leonard. We know
our plans for walls are laughable, our talk of women's
bodies, controlling, our attachment to guns,
suicidal, our intentions toward the indigenous,
soul-less. But we still need this empire, don't we?

For friends so long-standing they know
Where our ideas came from, gratitude.
For those younger who want our knowledge,
our experience, gratitude. For the moon
rising over Montreal whose wet
cobblestones shine like faces turned
toward the light, gratitude. The same
moon shines on a Manhattan tower.

In Montreal it ...

I.

In Montreal it rains straight up.

And down for hours at a time

On this rough-hewn stone hostel,

Still half-convent, its gated gardens

Shaded by catalpa inhabited

By crows who call out in driving rain

That ruins catalpa blossoms

And overruns the ancient gutters.

Grey Nuns pray for the river of humans

Running up St. Catherine

Ignoring the homeless

Dodging wind-twisted umbrellas.

Power resides in a crypt

Of three-hundred-year old stones

Containing remains of two hundred women

Who, praying, died of typhoid, polio

And cannot be exhumed so must be

Permanently sealed in place.

...rains straight up and down

II.

When the sun finally comes out
Over Mont Royal it means
Another hour of rain
But the sun is shining through
Its filaments connecting Earth
To the firmament.
And it makes me want to join
In all this praying
For the young man selling goat cheese
Rolled in ash at Jean Talon
For the berry-stained hands
For the fishy smells, the peaceful way
We gather our food and go home.
The mountain as the clouds clear
Is the prayer that will be heard
For the earth, its inhabitants
Waiting to be known as essential.

Thank You

To Neal, Betsy, and the Golden Antelope Press. To Laura Bigger for the cover: sometimes I have eyes but see not. To my assistant, Carly Walton for helping launch the book.

To Barbara for the gifts that would puzzle anyone but a writer. For the Annie Yeats print.

To Philip Tracy, RIP. They never arrested your murderer. I still feel that. Thank you for telling me the damage Honors English caused in metropolitan Detroit.

To Bob Dana, RIP. I will never forget your brown felt tip pen and the things it wrote in the margins of some people's poems. Okay, my poems.

For Susan Sage, Mike McColl, Mary Lou Docksey, and Deena Taylor: there should be plaques all over the Wayne State campus with our names on. We could start with the Belcrest Bar and Apartment Hotel, move on to Johnny's Dining Room, and arrive at the Bronx Bar and the lessons of the old poets: eventually you will be ticketed for loitering.

To Dudley Randall, RIP, and Broadside Press: for all those years putting Detroit on the literary map. I was in awe.

To Henrietta Epstein, RIP, for saying, "maybe you should read some Elizabeth Bishop."

To Gail for the early talks at the Park Street offices in Bloomington. For your exile on the prairie, next to my prairie, for the NWSAs, and the barefoot walks at Oval Beach.

To Sue Lafky, RIP, for teaching me that despite disaster and looming deadlines sometimes a journalist needs to help a feminist journal (*Feminist Teacher*) see the light of day. Thanks for moving pictures of men ("They haven't done anything noteworthy this week") to pg. 3 of the *Saturday Herald-Telephone*.

To my Splitrock Workshop mates for pointing out those were leaches on the bottoms of our feet at Gooseberry Falls, but it was nothing a smoked fish and a pie couldn't cure. To Linda Hasselstrom for the retreats at Windbreak House. I never saw cloudshadows big as a county before.

To Andrew for the many hours and for letting me dogsit your poetry books.

To Norma Jenckes for nodding and saying, "Maybe you should read some Anne Carson."

To Richard for never ordering books and then saying, "That book is readily available." Really?

To Allison Russel for sending me off with a book, *The New Basics*.

To Julia, for the tulip quilt. If you knew how many hours I have stared at it.

To my workshop mates at the Fine Arts Work Center. You may be underestimating yourselves.

To Jamie for the many hours. Why is it my porch rockers seem to collapse when you are sitting in them? I hear there's another supermoon coming up...

To Lori Desrosiers, if everything you do for poetry comes back to you even one-fold, you will be a rich woman.

To Seedlip.

To Clara Straight for making it to her 100th birthday by painting every day.

About the Author

Monica Barron writes poetry and nonfiction and has been a development editor for *Feminist Teacher* magazine and nonfiction selection editor for *wordpeace:* a digital social justice writing project. She helped launch Truman State University Press' Contemporary Nonfiction Book Series and served on the TSU Press Advisory Board. She is a member of the English faculty at Truman State University. Born in Michigan, she has never quite gotten the Great Lakes out of her system.

CPSIA information can be obtained
at www.ICGtesting.com
Printed in the USA
FSHW011618180220
67247FS